Managing Leadership

Stefan Kühl • Judith Muster

Managing Leadership

A Very Brief Introduction

Stefan Kühl
Universität Bielefeld
Bielefeld, Germany

Judith Muster
Universität Potsdam
Potsdam, Germany

Competing Interests The author has no competing interests to declare that are relevant to the content of this manuscript.

ISBN 978-3-032-09267-0   ISBN 978-3-032-09268-7   (eBook)
https://doi.org/10.1007/978-3-032-09268-7

Translation from the German language edition: "Führung managen" by Stefan Kühl and Judith Muster, © Der/die Herausgeber bzw. der/die Autor(en), exklusiv lizenziert an Springer Fachmedien Wiesbaden GmbH, ein Teil von Springer Nature 2025. Published by Springer Fachmedien Wiesbaden. All Rights Reserved.

Translation: Previously published with SN

This Springer imprint is published by the registered company Springer Nature Switzerland AG
The registered company address is: Gewerbestrasse 11, 6330 Cham, Switzerland

If disposing of this product, please recycle the paper.

Preface

The title of this book, *Managing Leadership*, may come as a surprise, as management and leadership are often simply set against each other in practical discourse (for early examples, see Zaleznik 1977; Zaleznik 1989; and, as one of many later imitations, Kotter 1990). According to the usual view, managers "manage," "maintain," and "imitate." They "accept the status quo," "focus on systems," and "rely on control." They are "rational and controlled," "have an eye to the bottom line," and "do things right." By contrast, leaders "innovate," "develop," and "create." They "challenge the status quo," "focus on people," and "rely on trust." They are "enthusiastic and inspiring," "have a vision in their hearts," and "do the right things" (in the ironical view of Neuberger 2002, p. 49).

In line with this, it has become fashionable to complain about an excess of management and a lack of leadership. Books, conferences, and training courses repeat like a mantra that there is too much management and too little leadership in organizations (for an example, see for a critical view McCann 2015, p. 173ff.). If you want to make a career in an organization, the impression is that you have to present yourself as a "charismatic leader" rather than an "administrative manager" (Gemmill and Oakley 1992, p. 114f.; Alvesson and Spicer 2014, p. 40).

The simple juxtaposition of leading and managing is indicative of the fact that most leadership approaches operate in an "organizational vacuum" (for an early critique, see Miner 1975; see also Lakomski 2005, p. 5). There is no systematic elaboration of how leadership relates to hierarchy. There is no analysis of the influence that programs in the form of if–then rules or targets have on leadership (see Türk 1981, p. 65). Even though leadership approaches that focused on the characteristics of leaders predominated for a long time, these characteristics were not linked back to the personnel component as a structural feature of organizations (see Türk 1987, p. 234f.)

The aim of this book is to bring the aspects of leadership into a closer relation with organizational dimensions, in contrast to the overly simplistic juxtaposition in practical discourse. In so doing, it will define the phenomenon of leadership in its various facets from a systems theory perspective. Precisely because the focus of the book is on leadership in organizations, it can only be accurately understood if one starts out by assuming that leadership occurs not only in organizations, but also in groups, movements, and families. This is the only way to recognize that claims to leadership can become entrenched in organizations in the form of hierarchies because members can be subjected to formal membership conditions.

It is not the intention of this book to provide small interactional tips and tricks that can be used to become more effective as a leader. At least since Niccolo Machiavelli's reflections on the subject were first published in the late middle ages, elaborate catalogs of behavior have been issued setting out the best way to lead (see Machiavelli 1955 and, for the transmission of Machiavelli's thought, Jay 1968;

McAlpine 2000; Bing 2004). Instead, this book is intended to help readers better understand leadership in an organizational context and, moreover, to enable them to identify trigger points for leadership, to recognize and shape occasions for leadership, to make leadership possible, or to reduce the outlay on it. To assume that leadership reduces uncertainty of expectation opens one's eyes to the fact that leadership always develops when the organizational structure offers too little support. This perspective not only provides an explanation for organizational situations in which there is a call for leadership, but also explains how the need for leadership can be reduced or increased by changing formal regulations.

This book is part of the continuously growing "Management Compact" series, in which the essentials for working in organizations are presented for the benefit of practitioners against the background of modern organizational theory. In addition to this volume, books on "Shaping organizations," "Influencing organizational culture," "Leading projects," "Developing strategies," "Developing mission statements," "Exploring markets," "Managing complexity," "Making Use of Management Fashions," and "Moderating workshops" have also been published. A book on "Lateral Leadership" presents the ways in which power, understanding, and trust affect the design of organizations. Because these books are based on the same fundamental ideas, attentive readers will find in them similar lines of thought and similar formulations. We deliberately use these overlaps to emphasize the unity of the underlying thought structure and the connections between the different books.

We do not believe in "simplifying" texts for managers and consultants by means of an assemblage of bullet points, executive summaries, and graphics. In many cases, readers are intellectually underchallenged by these aids because it is assumed that they are unable to extract the central ideas from a text without help. For this reason, we normally use a single graphic in books in this series to categorize the various topics—the meta-structure matrix. In this book, a second graphic is added because it illustrates our thoughts on the connection between organization and leadership—the management mixing console. In addition, we only use one element to make reading easier: small boxes. We use them on the one hand to provide empirical examples that illustrate our thoughts and on the other to mark detailed connections to organizational theory. If you are short of time, you can skip reading these boxes without losing the thread.

This book was developed as part of the Metaplan Professional program "Leading and Consulting in Discourse." We would like to thank the participants from various year groups who have not only critically questioned the approach presented here, but have also fed back their practical experience. We would also like to express our gratitude to the organizational scientists who have critically reflected and commented on Metaplan's practice on many occasions over the past few decades, particularly with regard to understanding leadership.

Universität Bielefeld   Stefan Kühl
Bielefeld, Germany   StefanKuehl@metaplan.com

Universität Potsdam   Judith Muster
Potsdam, Germany   judithmuster@metaplan.com

Contents

About the Authors

Stefan Kühl is Professor of Organizational Sociology at Bielefeld University and works as a consultant for Metaplan, particularly in dealing with ministries, administrations, companies, and associations.

Judith Muster is a partner at Metaplan and a research associate with the Chair of Organizational and Administrative Sociology at the University of Potsdam. She researches and advises on reorganization, leadership, and post-bureaucratic organization.

1

The Definition of a Chameleon Concept: Introduction

"Leadership" is one of the hardest terms to pin down in the world of organization. It seems to have almost as many definitions as there are people who have tried to define it (Stogdill 1974, p. 7). Looking at the many attempts at a definition in order to find something like a lowest common denominator, it would seem that leadership is all about directing the behavior of other people and seeing this directional role as a kind of permanent task to be undertaken by those in senior positions. In the vast majority of approaches to leadership, the focus is on the behavior of managers. It is they who, through their enactment of leadership, ensure the release of energy in the service of a common cause (Staehle 1985, p. 536), whose job is to inspire others or act as role models (Bass 1985). But it is almost impossible to identify a uniform, shared understanding of what leadership essentially is and what it is not in the jungle of different attempts to define leadership (on the difficulties of definition, see Pfeffer 1977, p. 104f.; Micklethwait and Wooldrige 1996, p. 168; Locke 2003, p. 29ff.).

© The Author(s), under exclusive license to Springer Nature Switzerland AG 2025
S. Kühl, J. Muster, *Managing Leadership*,
https://doi.org/10.1007/978-3-032-09268-7_1

The very vagueness of leadership makes it possible to load the term with a wide variety of hopes (see Witzel 2012, p. 400). Leadership is widely credited, for instance, with the ability to forge a community that will be capable of extraordinary achievements. Good leadership, it is thought, stops people feeling alienated from their work and makes them commit to it with great enthusiasm and passion. It is, apparently, the only way to ensure that instead of following well-trodden paths, people dare to take new ones. No matter what sort of problems arise in organizations, leadership is presented as the solution for each and every one (for a critical perspective, see Alvesson 2013, p. 170f.; Alvesson and Spicer 2014, p. 40).

Supposedly new approaches to leadership that can fulfil these hopes are therefore trotted out at regular intervals into the management concepts market. The term "leadership" is ideally suited to being turned into a concept straight away by being prefixed with a suitable adjective. Just add a modifier such as "authentic," "authoritarian," "charismatic," "cooperative," "situational," "strategic," "symbolic," "systemic," "transformational," or "visionary" and you have a catchy name for a leadership approach. This then just needs to be filled with appropriate principles, underpinned by scientific considerations, and supported with a few concrete tips for action, and there you have it—your own marketable leadership concept.

Managers and consultants seem to be irresistibly drawn to get involved in this game of inventing and propagating one new leadership concept after the other. You can, after all, make a name for yourself on the scene by becoming associated with one. Rhetorically sprucing up an already well-known concept is often enough to entitle you to put yourself forward as a keynote speaker on the management conference circuit. Quite a few managers are happy to pick up on the fashionable buzzwords, minimal reaccentuation, and colorful illustrations to avoid always having to repeat the same text when motivating their employees.

The problem, however, is that the knowledge gained in this ever-accelerating competition to invent new leadership concepts is extremely limited. Worse still, the verbiage associated with leadership is making it increasingly unclear what it is actually about. Sure, you could sit back and accept that the essence of leadership is to obscure what leadership is supposed to be. But it can also represent a gain in the sort of knowledge that is relevant to practice if the members of an organization can be clear about which aspects of their activities are being dealt with under the term leadership. That way leadership is transformed from a diffuse problem into one that can be shaped through good organization.

1.1 Leadership: A Systems Theory Definition

From a systems theory perspective, leadership can be understood as the successful exertion of an influence (see Luhmann 1964, p. 207ff.). Leadership presupposes that someone is willing to exert influence in a social situation and that others are willing to accept being influenced. The reasons for acceptance can vary greatly: attribution of competence, recognition of rhetorical skill, knowledge of a potential threat proceeding from mastery of sources of power, or even gratitude that someone is leading the way in an uncertain situation.

Leadership can therefore develop whenever it is unclear what is to be expected in a social interaction (for an early work on the subject, see Bavelas 1960, p. 492). In short: uncertainty of expectation is the precondition for the exercise of leadership. It can arise when there is general uncertainty about how to proceed, when written or unwritten rules leave a lot of room for interpretation, or when guide-lines need to be supplemented or replaced. If the traffic lights fail at a busy junction, someone has to take over con-trolling the traffic.

Leadership relies on a moment of uncertainty of expecta-tion. It requires a leadership impulse on the one side and a willingness to be led on the other. On the basis of this un-derstanding, it follows that anyone can lead in a social situ-ation as long as they are willing and able to "set the tone." If there is uncertainty among a group of friends about the best way to spend the evening, this can be reduced by one per-son persuasively explaining that they know of a new club and will be able get the group into it. Who this person is often only becomes clear through interaction within the group.

The exercise of leadership by a person can be limited to a one-off situation (Luhmann 1964, p. 208). It can happen that someone influences a decision in a situation of high uncertainty by making a contribution without there being any expectation that this person will take the lead again in the next similar situation. This is what we might call situa-tional leadership. If someone emerges as the spokesperson in a heated discussion, it does not necessarily mean that this person will be accorded the same importance in the next discussion. Situationally instigated leadership can easily collapse if it is not continuously reproduced by the finding of effective solutions.

This form of leadership develops particularly easily in unstructured situations among people who do not know one another. If certain individuals behave in a socially inap-propriate way at a party on the beach, strangers get into an argument during a train journey, or panic breaks out at a mass meeting, it can help to sort out the situation if one person takes the lead and this is accepted by the others pres-ent. However, because the likelihood of the same people meeting again is low, leadership will usually be limited to this one situation.

When people come together more often, leadership expectations—and therefore leadership demands—inevitably become more stable. If one particular person has regularly taken the lead in uncertain situations, the other people involved will expect this always to be the case and take a back seat. The person senses this expectation and therefore has better opportunities to assert a claim to leadership (Luhmann 1964, p. 208). They become the leader; the others become followers. Leadership expectations become institutionalized.

The institutionalization of leadership demands and expectations is particularly effective when it is secured from the outside. In modern society, many situations are characterized by the fact that it is predetermined who will take the lead when expectations are uncertain. In court, a judge is expected to take the lead in interactions when expectations are uncertain and not allow his or her authority to be disputed by prosecutors or defense attorneys, let alone defendants. Because their role is secured within the legal system and they have the means of violence at their disposal to back up their claims, judges have a good chance of enforcing their authority, although there is no guarantee that they will be able to do so. That depends on the situation.

1.2 Leadership: A Narrow Focus on Organizations

The need for leadership exists in different social structures, as there is no social system that is capable of offering complete certainty of expectation. Leadership can, therefore, be observed in social systems such as nuclear families, groups of friends, and protest movements, as well as in organizations. To focus on leadership in organizations, it is necessary to look at how certainty of expectation is produced in them. This is the only way of explaining how the expectational uncertainties develop that have then to be addressed by leadership.

Organizations differ from small families, groups of friends, and protest movements in that they generate formal expectations of their members. They are able to make membership subject to conditions and thus create conformist behavior among their members (Luhmann 1964, p. 29ff.). This forces the latter to accept orders, rules, and cooperation with often complicated colleagues—at least if they want to remain members of the organization. On this basis, organizations can formulate widely differing requirements that members must follow. The effect is that there are specific "triggers" for leadership in organizations.

Many management issues are triggered by conflicts of aims that are difficult to resolve once and for all in organizations. If the same software developers in a medium-sized software company are used both to working on existing projects and developing new business areas, a conflict of resources inevitably arises. The battle between the Chief Operations Officer and the Head of Business Development has to be "fine-tuned" by the management. Decisions must be made on a case-by-case basis as to whether resources should be made available for processing the old business or developing the new one. Leadership work is "programmed into" the organization because it is unable in principle to resolve conflicts of aims.

Further requirements for leadership arise when new demands are made on the organization. For example, uncertainty about expectations will develop when a customer makes new demands in a meeting and it is unclear whether and how these should be met. For a resourceful sales assistant, this kind of situation is an opportunity to send out a leadership impulse in the boss's direction while discussions are ongoing about what exactly the customer wants. The boss can, of course, simply refuse to follow that lead—and thereby create certainty that the firm will stick to its last and not adjust the product portfolio. However, he or she may also take up the sales assistant's suggestion because it seems plausible.

It can also happen in organizations that uncertainties are deliberately produced to allow new directions to be set through leadership. For example, programs that offer security may be ignored to enable leadership ambitions to come to light, or communication channels that provide orientation be bypassed to open up new opportunities for leadership. For example, a research and development manager sets up a critical juncture in a resource allocation meeting by announcing that the firm's own product is in danger of losing out in the next press ranking. He or she offers to solve the problem and is allocated the necessary resources. In this way, the existing development strategy negotiated with other departments is repeatedly undermined by leadership. However, because no one except the head of research and development has any insight into the way press rankings are drawn up, his or her lead is followed time and again.

We work with the meta-structure matrix to expound the expectation structure of organizations. Its—admittedly not exactly modest—aim is to capture all the ways in which expectations are created in organizations and to relate them to one another (Fig. 1.1).

In one dimension, we need to distinguish between the three forms in which expectations come into being in organizations. In simplified terms, we can speak of an

Managing leadership

	Communication channels	Programs	Personnel
Show side			
Formal side		Depending on the degree to which formal expectations are fixed and made effective, the need for and possibility of leadership will rise or fall.	
Informal side			

Fig. 1.1 The structural matrix for analyzing organizations

organization's show side, formal side, and informal side (for a brief account, see Kühl 2021, p. 88ff.).

The starting point for an analysis is the formal side, because this is only found in organizations. With the help of systems theory, it is possible to sum up the formal structures of an organization as its "already decided decision-making premises," the predetermined order that provides the premises on which further decisions are to be made and which the members of the organization must adhere to if they want to remain part of it. It is made up, for example, of the chain of command, reporting channels, co-signing rights, targets, or procedures that have been laid down by the organization in order to direct the behavior of its members. With a focus on leadership, it is particularly interesting to note how the mechanism of formality can be used to distribute leadership opportunities and resources within the organization.

Even so, it was noticed early on that there is always an informal side to organizations in addition to their formal side. The informal structure—the organizational culture—refers to expectations that are binding on members of the organization, but which are not flagged up as conditions of membership. These are expectations that have not been officially decided on but still structure members' actions. On this basis, informal structures in organizations can also be described as "undecided decision-making premises" (Luhmann 2000, p. 239) and include such things as short official channels, unwritten laws, functional deviations from rules and collegial expectations that nestle in the gaps of the formal structure. With leadership in mind, it is interesting to see the extent to which informal leadership roles develop in the shadow of the formal structure and which informal means of influence are used for leadership purposes. Think here in terms of people who do not feature prominently on the organizational chart but are nevertheless regularly consulted on issues, or of access to networks and the informational edge that goes along with it, which can be useful in ensuring people follow your lead in specific situations.

While for a long time it was assumed that the formal structure is the side that the organization presents to observers, the current assumption is that organizations always develop a "show side" in addition to their formal and informal sides (see Kühl 2021, p. 137ff.). This showcase structure consists of expectations whose only purpose is to gain legitimacy in the environment surrounding the organization. Elements of the formal structure may form part of it, but it often consists to a large extent of general-value formulations that make the organization appear attractive to the outside world. It only serves as a rough point of orientation for organizational members. Organizational facades of this kind do not simply exist, they have to be built up and expanded, regularly maintained and, if necessary, improved (Luhmann 1964, p. 113). The maintenance work can be seen in an organization's efforts to paint a positive picture of itself in mission statements, presentations, job advertisements and image ads. For example, even organizations with a whole series of hierarchical levels like to present themselves as having a fairly horizontal profile in their organization charts, while organizations in which senior management operates with quasi-military authority formulate sophisticated descriptions of collegial leadership for presentation at eye level.

The three sides have different degrees of relevance in relation to leadership in organizations. Leadership principles are set out on the show side: the values, that is, that stand for good leadership. On the formal side, people are appointed to supervisory roles thus determining who has authority and must be obeyed. Job descriptions are used to define what falls within the areas of responsibility of managers and employees and what does not. For example, creating a presentation may be part of a secretary's official range of tasks, whereas, formally speaking, getting birthday presents for the boss's children probably involves crossing a boundary. On the informal side, there are not only secret influencers whom you have to talk to if you want to get something done, for example, but also means of influence that you can use to assert your own claims to leadership.

Further insight can be acquired by focusing on the different types of structure that crystallize in organizations. Classification into communication channels, programs, and personnel has proved useful here (for the most extensive treatment, see Luhmann 2000, p. 256ff.). They can be observed not only on the formal side of the organization, but on the informal and the show sides as well.

The communication channels in organizations are particularly interesting as far as the question of leadership is concerned. Hierarchies, for example, determine the relationship between members. In terms of the formal structure, they define who can make claims on whom and who can expect to be followed. From looking at communication channels, however, it also becomes clear which leadership processes develop informally in the shadow of the formal structure. It is also interesting, from the same perspective, to see how an organization presents its decision-making channels to the outside world in order to acquire legitimacy within its environment.

The programs that operate inside organizations are also relevant to leadership issues, insofar as they define what can be done without making a mistake. They include rules, routines and strategies and provide certainty of expectation with regard to behavioral requirements. In this respect, they initially reduce the need for leadership. Authority has, for example, already been programmed into routines (Luhmann 1964, p. 98f.). It is clear that a work process has to be carried out in a set way. Routine relieves superiors of the situational exercise of their authority.

As a structural dimension, personnel determines which person or what kind of person fills a particular position. It matters whether generalists or technical experts are preferred as managers. If the best journalist is made editor-in-chief or the best engineer is made head of research and development, specialist knowledge remains a dominant influencing factor. It also makes a difference whether management positions are filled internally or externally. A member of staff who has spent their entire career in the organization can make use of the networks they have built up over the years, but is, at the same time, beholden to them. People who come from outside the organization have a freer hand but initially have no strong power base to rely on.

All the dimensions of the matrix are expectation structures whose task is to reduce uncertainty. But despite all attempts to create organizational structures, there is still a need for leadership in organizations, because not everything can be formalized. As a result, leadership turns out to be a product of the system that only becomes necessary when behavioral expectations are contradictory, unclear, or no longer adequate.

2

Leadership: Beyond a Purpose-Driven Understanding of the Organization

When people talk about leadership in organizations, there is usually an irritating limit to how far they go. When asked about the characteristics of leaders, they usually confine themselves to thinking about people who take on hierarchical positions. When leadership training courses are offered, the only members of the organization who can apply are those already in managerial positions or who will at least get to occupy them in the future. When people talk about leadership problems in an organization, they usually assume that senior staff are unable to get their employees to follow their instructions. In short, leadership is seen exclusively as influence exerted from above on those below—a top-down affair.

This restriction of leadership in organizations to leadership by superiors may seem immediately plausible in practice, but from a sociological point of view it comes as a surprise. If one assumes that leadership can shift around depending on the nature of the situation, it makes no sense that leadership in organizations should be monopolized by

© The Author(s), under exclusive license to Springer Nature Switzerland AG 2025
S. Kühl, J. Muster, *Managing Leadership*,
https://doi.org/10.1007/978-3-032-09268-7_2

particular individuals. There seems to be a mechanism in organizations that leads practitioners to think first and foremost of leadership by superiors, and the sociological idea that in principle any member can lead seems irritating.

How does this surprising restriction of leadership to the hierarchy come about and how does the mechanism that leads to leadership in organizations being expected solely of superiors actually work?

2.1   The Restriction of Leadership to the Hierarchy

Organizations could, in principle, leave the training and formation of leadership to the free play of circumstances. Leadership roles would shift continually from person to person depending on the situation: sometimes one would take the lead, sometimes the other. Expectations might creep in that the same person would always take the lead in situations of high uncertainty, thus forming a kind of informal hierarchy. However, this hierarchy would be very fragile and there would be no guarantee that it would be re-established with every new decision. There are organizations that try to experiment with a permanently fluctuating leadership. Anarchist grassroots organizations, religious sects, and start-ups in the early growth phase are examples of organizations that try to prevent formalized hierarchies. It is not uncommon for organizations of this kind in particular to very rapidly develop pronounced informal hierarchies in which certain individuals exercise extreme influence on decision-making but cannot, however, be held clearly responsible for the decisions arrived at (for well-documented religious and political examples, see Lalich 2004; for economic examples, Laloux 2014).

But even if there are individual attempts by organizations to dispense with formalized rankings (see, for example, Nutzinger 1979), the vast majority of organizations still rely on hierarchies as a mechanism for formalizing leadership. Even if attempts are made to conceal hierarchies by means of visual representations in the form of pie charts instead of organizational charts, by inverting organizational pyramids, or through servant leadership campaigns, there is hardly an organization that does without them.

All organizations develop a formal hierarchy in one form or another, at least if the organization is large enough that not all employees can fit around a kitchen table. In some organizations, hierarchies are easy to recognize because they are depicted in their organizational charts and members therefore have no difficulty in determining exactly who their own superiors are, as defined by the hierarchy, and which employees are hierarchically subordinate to them. Other organizations conceal the hierarchy by presenting themselves as boss-free companies, but the employees know exactly who holds how much capital in the company and can therefore, in fact, exercise the role of boss at any time.

2.1.1 The Generalizing Power of Hierarchies

The key feature of hierarchies is that leadership claims in organizations do not have to be renegotiated every time, but are generalized in temporal, factual, and social terms (for the authoritative account, see Luhmann 1964, p. 161 f.). Generalization refers to the process by which a particular arrangement is made independent of individual events, freed from the vicissitudes of people's form on the day, and immunized against breakdowns (Luhmann 1964, p. 55 f.). This may sound complicated at first glance, but it quickly becomes clear when you look in detail at how leadership claims are generalized in hierarchies (on what follows below, see Kühl 2021, p. 68ff.).

Hierarchies ensure a *temporally* unlimited willingness to follow. Although temporary leadership structures do exist for deputies, interim managers, or project-related management roles, members of the organization can generally assume that the hierarchical order is permanent. The manager today will most likely still be manager tomorrow. It will surprise no-one if the person who gives instructions today continues to allocate tasks such as preparing a report, planning a meeting, or even fetching the coffee the following day. Conversely, members of the organization would react with great irritation if managers suddenly stopped behaving in accordance with their role.

The hierarchy also clearly defines who is *socially* subordinate to whom in the organization. A hierarchically structured organizational chart establishes essential social relationships between all members. Organizational charts thus help to coordinate the behavior of members of the organization. It is true that it occasionally happens in organizations that members are unsure which manager they report to or there is a lack of clarity about who is responsible for a particular member. However, such uncertainties in social assignment can usually be clarified quickly. If contradictions or ambiguities persist in the assignment of members, it is the responsibility of the higher authority to ensure clarification and order.

The hierarchy also organizes *functional* responsibilities within the organization. This happens both horizontally, i.e. between the departments at the same hierarchical level, and vertically, between different levels. In principle, there is the option for issues to be escalated upwards from the lower levels. Although managers should only intervene in exceptional cases and take on responsibilities that are actually decentralized, they always retain the fundamental option and formal right to take over any decision-making situation at the lower levels and transform it into a top priority area.

How does this generalization of leadership claims come to be generally accepted in organizations?

2.1.2 Recognition of the Organizational Hierarchy as a Condition of Membership

The stability of leadership structures in organizations is ensured by making acceptance a prerequisite for membership. Anyone who joins an organization and wishes to remain part of it is required to follow the instructions of their manager, even if the logic behind a specific instruction is not immediately obvious. The effectiveness of this principle can be illustrated by a simple experiment in crisis management: All you have to do is tell your superior that you will no longer follow their instructions in the future. The subsequent reactions within the organization impressively illustrate the strength of the formalization mechanism.

Because hierarchy enables organizations to decide in principle who is in charge and from whom obedience is required, they are relieved of the burden of negotiating leadership on a situational basis. To this end, the role of superiors is defined and what this entails is formally laid down. Job descriptions and organizational charts define who can demand obedience from whom and to what extent. It is no longer the convincingly presented argument or the promise of consideration that counts, but simply the superior's position. This has an important consequence for the understanding of leadership: if instructions are carried out without further ado, this is not a case of leadership— merely of a functioning hierarchy. If a boss instructs an assistant to book a flight and the assistant books it, this is not an enactment of leadership. There is never any uncertainty about who will book the flight: who receives instructions and who gives them.

Very often, however, situations arise in which hierarchy does have to be enforced through leadership. Formal instructions are not always recognized and implemented. The secretary might have good reasons for not making the flight booking today—a strike at the airport, a better way of using his resources, or a deadline that is still unclear. When the assistant presents these reasons, there is initial uncertainty about how the right decision should be made. The instruction from the hierarchy is countered by a factual justification. Only now does the opportunity arise for either party to take the lead. The boss can assert herself by reference to her hierarchical position—in that case she takes the lead and has to live with the canceled flight or the missed appointment. The assistant can also assert himself with his arguments—in that case he takes the lead and has to live with the fact that he was right, but also refused to follow. "As a member of the leadership of an organization, one cannot," to Niklas Luhmann's way of thinking (1964, p. 37) "refuse to follow instructions without laying claim to leadership oneself." In many cases, situations arise in which superiors have to exercise leadership in order to force their instructions through. Leadership becomes necessary despite the generalized power provided by the hierarchy and thus becomes an *additional* source of power within the system through which influence can be exerted in certain situations.

2.1.3   The Advantages of Generalized Leadership Claims

The condition of accepting hierarchy as part of membership has a significant effect: leaders do not necessarily have to rely on the personal esteem in which they are held by their subordinates as the basis for their influence (see Luhmann 1964, p. 209). Nor do they any longer need to explain the logic behind an instruction in every situation—regardless of whether it has to do with carrying out a risky military action, developing an innovative spread to put on a slice of bread, or fighting a tricky legal case against copyright infringement. This gives the organization the opportunity to put staff in leadership positions if they are technically qualified but not born charismatic.

This idea—of being relieved through the hierarchy of the necessity of earning the respect of one's subordinates—usually leads to fierce protests from advocates of modern management concepts. If the founder of an Internet mail order company and the management team help out on the assembly lines at one of the firm's logistics centers during the Christmas rush, this is a clear sign of how important it is to act as a role model for one's subordinates. According to the leadership literature, managers who are only respected because of their hierarchical position, but not because of who they are as people, can achieve nothing in the organization. Any experience with organizations will show that one has to convince one's subordinates of the meaningfulness of individual instructions. The concept of charismatic, transformational leadership, which pops up again from time to time, starts at precisely this point. It assumes that only a rousing, transformational leadership style is capable of developing the true potential of employees.

Of course, there is little to be said against employees showing personal respect for their superiors or carrying out instructions because they are convinced that they are correct. But this will often only be the case during an organization's fine-weather phases, when business is going well, no drastic restructuring measures are necessary, and employees are sure of their jobs. Organizations could not exist in the long term if their members were only willing to follow a lead if they were personally carried away by their superiors or if they immediately recognized the meaningfulness of the instructions they were given. Besides, this demand for charismatic leadership overtaxes managers who come from specialist careers as well as employees who are constantly exposed to motivational speeches from managers.

In idealized concepts of the organization, market orientation, the customer, or the law is always linked to a desire to promote the well-being of each individual employee. In ceremonial speeches, company executives and heads of public authorities regularly emphasize that "motivated and inspiring employees" are the central element in achieving "satisfied customers." Trade union representatives also state —albeit following a slightly different line of argument—that achieving the goals of companies, administrative bodies, prisons, and military units is not only possible through appropriate remuneration for work, but also through employees having a positive attitude towards their organization.

Organizational life, however, is not a bowl of cherries. A supervisor cannot be focused primarily on the "benevolently authoritative" care of his or her employees, but must also take into account the requirements of customers, clients, or constituents (Luhmann 1964, p. 210). The needs brought to bear on the organization from "without" often come into conflict with the expectations expressed from "within"—by the employees. Clients strive for the most cost-effective services possible; employees expect fair remuneration for their work. Ideally, clients demand constant availability from the organization; employees want their working hours to be limited.

Hierarchies allow organizations to adapt to external demands without always having to consider the sensitivities of their members. Companies have the opportunity to decide which markets they want to enter without necessarily having to consider whether their employees are willing to relocate for these projects. Ministries can focus on which draft legislation offers the best way to implement reforms, without having to consider whether the departmental specialists are pursuing the same political line.

By reducing managers' need to rely on the "personal respect" of their employees, hierarchies give them the freedom to make unpopular decisions that break through existing expectations (see Luhmann 1964, p. 209; Luhmann 2000, p. 322). This enables management, for instance, to relocate production facilities abroad without the consent of the workforce. They are also allowed to implement new production processes even if this devalues the expertise of long-serving employees.

The ability of hierarchies to enable new beginnings within organizations is particularly evident by comparison with those organizations that, for political reasons or due to an inability to remunerate their members, are unable to fall back on hierarchical structures. Such organizations tend to cling to the status quo. It is often difficult for them to make fundamental changes. By contrast, as empirical organizational research has shown, organizations with strong hierarchies have a greater ability to implement far-reaching changes more quickly and effectively (see March and Simon 1958, p. 194ff.; Luhmann 1964, p. 209).

Emphasis on Formality or Informality in Management Discourse

Two fundamentally different ideas of structural formation can be distinguished in management discourse. In the one, attempts are made to achieve efficiency, effectiveness, and innovation in organizations through a maximum degree of formality, while in the other, a maximum degree of informality is used to achieve these goals. If one is to be guided by the preference in management literature for model designations reduced to one letter—"Model X", "Model Y", "Model J" and so on—then one might speak at this point of a "Model F" and a "Model I" as the dominant variants in management discourse (cf. Kühl 2023).

The aim of "Model F" is to formalize as many of the behavioral expectations applicable to members of the organization as possible through precise role definitions. The recipe for success is seen in ever greater detailing and perfecting of formal role expectations. The existence in organizations of informal expectations to which people are subject is acknowledged, but the aim is to translate as many of these as possible into formal ones. According to the traditional depiction, people should function like cogs in the organizational gearbox. Consequently, the metaphors used for this model are those of a machine, a mechanism, an apparatus, or an operating system (cf. Morgan 1986, p. 19ff.).

"Model I", on the other hand, relies on the fact that as many expectations as possible come into being informally in organizations on the basis of personal trust (see, for example Toffler 1971; Mintzberg and McHugh 1985; Peters 1993; Ciborra 1996). The formula for success consists of resisting the urge to formalize behavioral expectations more and more through progressively more detailed job descriptions. The necessity of formal role expectations is not negated, but these should merely form a framework for informal expectations based on personal trust. In short, people should be at the heart of the organization. The metaphors used for this organizational model are those of an organism, a community, a lifeworld, or a culture (cf. Morgan 1986, p. 39ff.).

It is very clear to see how leadership models focus on the potential of either formality or informality. Not only is the history of organizational concepts described as an alternation between formality and informality, the history of leadership concepts is too. Sometimes leadership concepts are directly linked to the organizational ones, sometimes they are introduced into the discussion independently of them.

In the formality-oriented leadership model, Model F, the strength of leadership in an organization is emphasized through the commitment of all its members to hierarchical directives. It is conceded that it can be helpful to inspire enthusiasm for the goals of the organizations, to develop visions, and to be responsive to employees, but ultimately superiors can rely on the fact that following their instructions is part of the formal conditions of membership (on legal rule as a type, see Weber 1976, p. 124ff.). The terms used to designate people in formally elevated leadership roles are boss, chief, superior, or executive.

In the informality-oriented leadership model, Model I, the emphasis is on leaders inspiring their followers (for a critical account, see Yukl 1999). They should make the meaning, the purpose, of their activities clear to them, clarify their vision of the future of the organization, and motivate them. At the same time, the followers' needs must not be lost sight of. The fact that leadership in organizations is generally supported by integration into a formal authority structure is tacitly assumed, rather than considered central to the enforcement of expectations. This concept is expressed in designations of people in leadership roles as advisor, coach, role model, teacher, or servant (cf. Bass 1985, p. 27).

The concept of Taylorism at the beginning of the twentieth century, combined through-programming of work processes with the formal authority of superiors to issue instructions. As a reaction against Taylorism in the early decades of the twentieth century, the concept of the *Werkgemeinschaft*, i.e. the ideology of the National Socialist works community and the organizational concept of human relations, embodied the idea that leadership is based on the characteristics of outstanding people. Charismatic leadership, following the example of political and religious movements, was one term for this. In more formal management models based on target agreements—keyword: transactional leadership—the function of superiors consisted in the formulation of formally binding targets and the monitoring of their achievement. It emphasized that leadership does not depend on charisma and that many famous leaders have in fact had surprisingly little charisma (on this point, see Drucker 1982). Then, with the emphasis again on organizational culture, aspects such as the power of vision, the ability to inspire, the role model function and the caring ability of superiors were highlighted. Because the term charismatic leadership had become obsolete, not least due to its association with National Socialism, terms such as inspirational, visionary, or transformational leadership were invented to replace it.

2.2   The Blind Spot When Reducing Leadership to Hierarchy

The concept of leadership based on hierarchy is an expression of the purpose-driven understanding of organizations. It assumes that enacting leadership contributes first and foremost to the "purpose" of the organization. In the end, according to this view, this primary purpose is the reason for the organization's existence and the guiding principle behind all organizational action. Regardless of what the purpose of the organization is—the manufacture of washing machines, the processing of pension applications, the detention of criminals, or the implementation of further climate protection measures—according to this understanding, the raison d'être of organizations *is only* seen in the fulfilment of that purpose.

2.2.1   The Parallel Connection of Purpose and Hierarchy Structure

In accordance with this understanding of organizations, their main goal can be broken down into several subgoals. This makes it possible to create complex chains of ends and means within organizations, in which each end serves only as a means to fulfil another higher-level goal. This goal, in turn, is only one element in a sequence of further goals.

In this simplified view of organizations, every purpose—whether a main, an intermediate, or a subordinate purpose—is assigned to a specific position within the hierarchy. The structure of purposes and means is thus synchronized with the hierarchical structure (cf. Weber 1976, p. 125). The managers at the highest level determine how the organization is to achieve its goals. The necessary actions to be undertaken as means to the end in question are then assigned as tasks to subordinate employees. They in turn pass on partial tasks to the next lower levels until the lowest level of the hierarchy, i.e. the direct labor level, is reached. The hierarchical structure thus merely reflects the "order of ends and means" within an organization (see Luhmann 1973, p. 73).

2.2.2 Overlooking the Consequential Problems of Leadership

The "parallel connection" between the ends-and-means relation and a series of hierarchical distinctions running top to bottom makes for clear organizational analyses that have little to do with organizational reality. With the focus on hierarchy, leadership in the true sense is even lost from view. The organization appears to be a machine that is organized end to end with managers as one of many cogs within it. This overlooks the subtle tactics, the little tricks of the trade, and the more or less skillful maneuvers that are part of leadership and are needed to keep organizations running despite their structures. The leadership requirements that have developed in the shadow of the hierarchy are neglected. Thus, a purpose-driven understanding of organizations not only obscures the necessity of leadership, but also loses sight of its consequential problems, overlooking the fact that, although leadership in organizations reduces uncertainty in principle, it is also an uncertain mechanism for providing solutions for the organization itself.

In terms of the first of these follow-up problems, leadership is an activity that brings about a change in orientation that is motivated by means of people. Those who lead must present their audience with credible offers that make following them appear as a logical consequence. The success of such offers is closely bound up with who or what these people are. People in leadership roles must appear credible to their audience for a variety of reasons. Many means of influence are closely linked with them: Charisma, personal connections, and the instinct for finding the appropriate words at the appropriate time play a decisive role. But the organization itself can also provide appropriate support, such as control over resources and access to information or customers. However, whether the right means can be mobilized in a particular management situation depends solely on the people involved. They must sense the uncertainty of expectations, select a leadership option, and bring the means of influence to bear. To do this, in case of doubt they must be sufficiently alert, in the right place, in the right situation, and not distracted by private problems or incoming messages on their cell phone.

Organizations, as far as the second consequential problem is concerned, ultimately have no control over who takes the lead in practice. They may officially appoint "leaders," but a quick glance at their diaries is often enough to raise the question of who is actually leading whom. In any briefing that summarizes complex content in ten PowerPoint slides, or when the top level of the hierarchy is presented with three carefully selected options and simply responds with "We're going for option C!", leadership does take place, but from the bottom up, not the other way around. Overall, the value of hierarchies for leadership purposes is often overestimated. Organizations may make it mandatory that certain members have the authority to make decisions in open situations, but if team leaders have to emphasize their leadership by highlighting the position they occupy, they are mainly showing how little they actually contribute to the way that processes function.

An essential characteristic of leadership as something accomplished in a situation is the third consequential problem: its transience. Even in cases where the same problems recur, the need for guidance can arise again and again if that can only be guaranteed by leadership and is not already built in. For managers, this manifests itself in the typical "We've been over this before" discussions. For those who require guidance, however, leadership does not yet appear to be available in a clear form, so that no transition to routine is possible. This is the challenge of leadership: the impetus must be constantly renewed. Where problems persist and leadership can only offer a one-off solution for each occurrence, there is initially only a situational solution to the problem.

What would an understanding of leadership look like that, on the one hand, recognizes the formalization of influence in the form of hierarchies, but at the same time recollects that a wide variety of forms of leadership can develop in the shadow of the hierarchy?

2.3 The Three Directions of Leadership in Organizations

If one understands the relatively loose coupling of leadership and hierarchy, it is possible to observe in organizations a number of very different leadership directions that are otherwise easily overlooked. The focus on hierarchy in mainstream leadership literature means that although the top-to-bottom order that exists in every large organization gets considered, authors overlook the fact that leadership is not only possible top-down, but also along the same hierarchical level and even from the bottom up.

2.3.1 Lateral Leadership: Leadership on a Level

Organizational research recognized early on that, in addition to hierarchical structures, lateral leadership, i.e. leadership between members of an organization at the same hierarchical level, plays an important role in companies, public authorities, hospitals, and non-governmental organizations. The more diverse and dynamic the environment of an organization—the faster markets, knowledge levels, and political conditions change—the more organizations tend to decentralize. In such a context, hierarchical control mechanisms lose influence, while lateral forms of cooperation become increasingly important (as argued by Burns and Stalker 1961; Lawrence and Lorsch 1967).

Lateral leadership aims to enforce behavioral expectations in situations where no authority to issue instructions is possible, where no hierarchy is available. Such situations often occur in projects in which different areas are involved, but in which even the project management has no hierarchical authority over the subordinate areas. Consider such situations as a company-wide introduction of software, a cross-divisional reorganization, or the implementation of a global digital strategy. However, lateral leadership can also occur in day-to-day business, for example when someone has to communicate in the context of processes that cross departmental boundaries or when a multidimensional matrix no longer reflects classic superordinate and subordinate structures. In the absence of clear organizational super- and subordinates, influence is often exerted via exchange, common interests, or power (for a detailed study, see Kühl 2017).

It should not be overlooked that, inside organizations, lateral leadership usually takes place within a basic hierarchical structure. When analyzing these processes, it becomes clear that, on the one hand, the directive power of the hierarchy is insufficient to set processes in motion or make decisive decisions, though the hierarchy continues to serve as a point of reference. Even if lateral cooperation partners are reluctant to involve it, the course of power games, the development of relationships of trust, and communication processes can (also) be shaped by the involvement of the hierarchy, which is possible in principle.

2.3.2 "Undersight" of the Overseers: Leadership by Subordinates

A second direction of leadership operates through the hierarchy, but from the bottom up. In sociology, this is referred to as "supervising the supervisors from below" (Luhmann 2016). Senior ranks may restrict the scope of action of their subordinates, but they also necessarily allow themselves to be used by them for the latter's own interests. Subordinates use their superiors to project their own behavioral expectations upwards. This is because superiors are an important and "versatile tool for subordinates in the implementation of plans and intentions." Superiors serve as "amplifiers and shock absorbers" (Luhmann 2016, p. 90).

Supervising superiors from below requires a high level of skill on the part of subordinates. Coordination with peers is crucial to focus the attention of superiors. Unified action among employees can strengthen control over the presentation of problems to management. The influence to hand is based on an ability to presort information and contribute expertise. Subordinates use their expertise and control over information to guide decisions and, if necessary, to pass problems upwards in a targeted manner. Evaluating means of influence helps one to have the right levers within reach in leadership situations. Strategic action requires sensitivity, as formal decision-making power remains with the line manager. Through skillful supervision, embedded in trust-based cooperation, managers can be effectively led "on a long leash" without directly undermining their authority.

"Undersight" does not cancel out the hierarchy, it makes use of it. As bargaining chips, employees have the means to make their managers' everyday lives easier. If managers largely meet the expectations of their employees, they can count on their cooperation and support in day-to-day management. Particularly well-supervised supervisors may get mocked by top management as "class reps." However, if management rejects initiatives from below, employees may withhold their cooperation and commitment and pass on any unresolved problems to the top. In such cases, management would quickly become overburdened and be forced to resume contact with their employees. The possibility of leading from the bottom up is based on the threat of over-burdening the hierarchy with decision-making. The sober truth is: without the active support of their subordinates, managers would quickly sink into chaos.

The concept of "undersight" dispels the widespread misconception that means of influence are to be found primarily at the top of the hierarchy, while those at the bottom are increasingly powerless. Running counter to the formal hierarchy, there are various leadership opportunities that convey behavioral expectations from the bottom to the top. Supervision from below thus contributes significantly to the performance of organizations, but it is not something that can be relied on in a formal setup. Subordinates have the formal right to stop leading their superiors at any time and to invoke the hierarchy.

2.3.3 Changing Lanes: Typical Occasions for Leadership by Superiors

Of course, the dominant direction of leadership in management literature also occurs empirically: Supervisors do lead, from the top down. It is not uncommon for them to have to enforce their expectations as leaders. Typical occasions for exercising leadership despite occupying a senior position are when implementing new formal expectations, when replacing informal behavior with formal rules, and when realizing informal expectations.

Organizations often need leadership when informal behaviors are to be replaced by formal ones. The informal behaviors in question may either have previously been tolerated or the manager may have previously been unaware of them. This change of track from an informal back to the formal expectation structure is particularly difficult for supervisors because actions in the area of "usable illegality" remain latent (Luhmann 1964, p. 304). When asked "Do you keep to the rules?", the supervisor will presumably always answer "yes." Furthermore, simply repeating the rules overlooks the function of deviating from the rules, which can possibly close gaps in them, enable faster coordination, or even improve processes. Managers must find other solutions to these problems that are compatible with the formal structure and support them with situational leadership.

Managers also often rely on informal leadership opportunities to implement goals that are not formally required but are nevertheless essential to the success of the organization. Consider, for example, the fact that sales managers persuade their employees to soften the rules they have set for dealing with new customers in certain cases. This is a tricky game for managers, because on the one hand they have to ensure that rules are not eroded, while, on the other, they depend on being able to interpret them flexibly. Informal mechanisms are a way of securing compliance with mechanisms that are formally illegal: for example, when managers smoke in the workplace despite a smoking ban, allow illegal barbecues to go ahead on company premises or bill communal lunches as business entertainment. In this way, expectations of managerial behavior can be shaped that cannot be derived from the hierarchy and even contradict it in some cases. For senior staff, this presents opportunities; they have something to offer: "The very fact that these important and highly desirable services cannot be formalized and cannot be demanded, but have to be freely supplied provides the starting point for the development of elementary leadership activities in the shadow of the formal rankings" (Luhmann 1964, p. 212). Forms of exchange arise between managers and employees that can lead to enhanced performance.

New Formal Expectations Are to be enforced: The Case of a Technology Group

In one technology group, we observed that one reorganization followed hard on the heels of another. The group was caught between the conflicting priorities of staff reduction targets and the protection afforded to employees by collective bargaining. Reorganizations were the means of choice to justify staff cuts. Members of the organization had become accustomed to the fact that, although reorganizations came with glittering announcements of better working conditions, they ended up with more work for fewer people. It was impossible to talk openly about this within the group.

A few years later, when a reorganization was actually not driven by staff cuts but was supposed to make new business models possible in line with technological progress, nobody really believed the promises. The employees in the departments concerned accepted the new matrix structure without resistance, but effectively ignored it. On the quiet, we were told: "We're going sit out the matrix. It's not meant seriously anyway." What to do when a reorganization has been formally announced, but no one complies with it? All that was left was laborious, repeated situational leadership efforts to establish and enforce the new structure in individual interactions, until the expectations of the members of the organization had been realigned.

Means of Influence

In organizations, a lot of thought is typically given to who should take the lead. Relatively little thought is given to how the relevant people are to be provided with the resources for exercising leadership. A classic conflict between top and middle management occurs when top management expects leadership from middle management—but the latter announces that it has too little influence. To be able to generate followership in situations where expectations are uncertain, means of influence are needed.

Niklas Luhmann refers to mechanisms that can be used to enforce behavioral expectations on others as *means of influ-*

ence (Luhmann 1964, p. 132). Means of influence increase the probability that others will adopt the behavioral expectations that have been communicated to them. These means of influence can either be derived from the formal structure of the organization (e.g. leave approvals or authority to issue instructions), have their origin in informal structures (e.g. membership of certain organizational cliques or networks), or are characteristics of a person (e.g. charisma). Not all of these means of influence can simply be "organized" by the organization. Charismatic character traits are difficult to train through personnel development measures, and informal access to resources cannot be decided by the organization. Nevertheless, a large part of the means of influence available for leadership are predetermined by the structures of the organization or can be influenced by it, for example, through communication processes.

Which means of influence are available depends on the organization in question. It is therefore impossible to compile a list of means of influence. It is, however, possible to devise theory-based search criteria that make the distribution of means of influence within the organization visible and accessible to manipulation.

Crozier and Friedberg (1977) identified typical sources from which influence might flow and called them zones of uncertainty, because influence is largely based on its being uncertain whether those who have it will choose to exercise it. The hierarchy-based influence possessed by senior staff relies on their ability to issue formal organizational rules that can restrict or expand subordinates' fields of action. The means of influence available to them therefore depend largely on the decision-making powers they have. Can they grant time off work, can they change work processes or team relationships, are they the ones who put together shifts or is this done centrally by HR? Structural decisions such as these also determine the organization's means of influence and therefore distribute leadership opportunities. However, hierarchies also allow subordinates to exert influence: by overburdening the hierarchy with unresolved problems over time (Luhmann 2016).

IT or marketing specialists gain their influential positions from their mastery of *expert knowledge* that is relevant to the organization. Expertise and specialization that are difficult to replace provide important means of influence. How knowledge is distributed and made accessible within the organization has a lot to do with who can exert influence in situations where expectations are uncertain.

Staff who act as *relay points* to the environment have means of influence because they have privileged access to customers, central suppliers, important cooperation partners or influential government agencies. How access is structured in these cases, whether it is centralized or available to several members of the organization, plays a decisive role in determining who has a good chance of leading.

A final source of influence results from the control of important internal communication channels and sources of information. So-called *gate keepers*, for example, secretaries or personal advisors, acquire advance information that they can use as influence in management situations. How unique and therefore influential such access to information is will be determined by the formal communication channels.

If you want to take a look at the distribution of means of influence in your own organization, you can ask yourself, for example: What decision-making powers does the hierarchy possess? What limits the decision-making powers of the hierarchy? How is knowledge distributed within the organization? Who needs what kind of access to expert knowledge? How is access to important players in the environment organized? Who needs what sort of advance information or communication channels to generate influence?

The answers to these questions provide information about which leadership opportunities are made available to whom by the organization. However, whether a means of influence actually generates influence and prompts followership will depend on the specific situation, the relevance of the problem, and the interaction skills of those involved.

3

Management Substitutes: On the Mixing Desk of the Organization

A great deal of the leadership literature deals with tricks, big and small, that a person can use to influence decisions through skillful leadership. It explains how managers can act as motivating communicators, convincing problem solvers and popular leaders (Jachtchenko 2021) how leaders are able to achieve extraordinary things through close relationships with their employees (Kouzes and Posner 2017) and how more feeling can unleash the power of emotional intelligence in organizations (Goleman et al. 2013).

There is nothing wrong with this mixture of stories about successful leaders, examples of problems from leadership practice, small tips for conducting conversations, and tools for resolving conflicts. Because leadership is based to a considerable extent on successful influence in interactions such as conversations, meetings, or workshops, it helps to acquire one or two interactional skills. Books on leadership, presentations at conferences, and seminars with reflections on one's own impact can reinforce the idea that leadership is not limited by one's own personality developed over many years, but that one can acquire promising skills and competencies even at a more or less advanced age.

For all the usefulness of these tips and tricks, the organizational leverage of these interaction-based measures is low. The books, presentations, and seminars on the subject of leadership interaction may give individuals confidence, from which subordinates, colleagues, and superiors may benefit as well. People at the top in particular can achieve wide-ranging effects within the organization, because leadership styles are often copied by subordinates. Ultimately, however, this support is only aimed at the interaction skills of individuals.

From the point of view of an approach informed by organizational theory, it is therefore especially interesting to see how the design of organizational structures influences the possibilities of, and demands on, leadership. The question here is how can the conditions of leadership be influenced by a change in the formal structures of the organization. Headings under which answers to this question tend to be sought are "Substitutes for leadership in organizations" (Kerr 1977, p. 135ff.; Kerr and Jermier 1978, p. 377f.), "Mechanisms of depersonalized leadership" (Türk 1981, p. 67f.; Türk 1987, p. 234f.) or "Functional equivalents for leadership in organizations" (Luhmann 1964, p. 207).

The basic idea behind these approaches, all of which are informed by organizational theory, is simple. Because the degree of expectational uncertainty varies, the need for leadership varies as well. If there is no uncertainty of expectation, no pressure to act, there is hardly any need for leadership. If the behavior of pedestrians, cyclists, and motorists is clearly regulated by traffic lights, there is no need for someone to direct the traffic. Conversely, a high degree of uncertainty makes the call for leadership louder. There are opportunities to take the lead and thus reduce the uncertainty.

If the traffic lights fail due to a technical breakdown, the resultant uncertainty can be reduced through leadership.

The concept of management substitutes embodies the idea that there are opportunities in organizations to influence the degree of expectation uncertainty. The lever for regulating it is the precision with which formal expectations can be fixed and enforced. If every behavioral expectation of the members of the organization can be precisely determined by leadership substitutes, the need for leadership in the organization will be low. However, if precisely differentiated behavioral expectations cannot be perfectly catered for in practice because everyday life turns out to be completely different from what was anticipated in the planning, then the need for leadership increases again. If it proves impossible to fix behavioral expectations via leadership substitutes, the need for leadership increases.

In research, various leadership substitutes have been listed (see, for example, Türk 1987, p. 238f.): the professional orientation of employees, wages that vary according to performance, the precise formulation of tasks, technically secured feedback on performance, detailed process descriptions. Such lists provide an overview of the variety of organizational phenomena that can be used to reduce the need for management. However, additional insights can be obtained if a distinction is made between the central types of organizational structure—programs, communication channels, and personnel—when looking at leadership substitutes. In principle, what cannot be accomplished in organizations through structures must be achieved through leadership. The question as to which leadership requirements will likely arise in an organization and which will not can be shaped to a large extent by structural decisions. Structural decisions, though, can in turn lead to problems that need to be anticipated when those decisions are taken.

3.1 The Replacement of Leadership by Programs

Programs bundle criteria according to the nature of the decisions that have to be made. They determine what can and cannot be done in an organization. In this respect, programs have the function of assigning responsibility for mistakes and thus distributing blame within the organization. If an employee does not achieve the target of a 10% increase in turnover set by a program, he or she may look for excuses, but ultimately programming enables the error to be laid in the first instance at his or her door. In organizations, there are two fundamentally different types of program: conditional ones and purpose-oriented ones (cf. March and Simon 1958, p. 164ff.).

3.1.1 Different Forms of Program

Conditional programs lay down what has to be done if a particular occurrence is perceived to have taken place in an organization. An operative makes a mistake if the prescribed work step is not carried out when the occurrence is detected, and can be held accountable for this. Conversely, if the program is followed correctly, it is not the operative who is responsible for the outcome of the work process, but the developer of the program. If an administrative employee processes an application correctly, he or she will not be held accountable for what happens when the program is applied.

Purpose-oriented programs, on the other hand, specify which goals or purposes are to be achieved. Purpose programs are often found at the top of an organization, for example when the manufacture of bicycles is stated to be the purpose of a company or a nongovernmental organization states that its purpose is the prohibition of a certain type of landmine. However, they are also used further down in the organization for structuring purposes. In purpose-oriented programs, unlike conditional ones, the choice of means is free: The stated purpose is to be achieved, no matter how. The choice of means must remain within the limits set by the rules of the organization or by legal regulations. The rule of thumb is: Any means that is not prohibited by the organization (or by law) is permitted to achieve the goal.

3.1.2 Programs and Leadership

The behavior of people in organizations is regulated by programs (for the basics see Simon 1957; March and Simon 1958). Particularly when tasks are highly repetitive or goals can be specified in detail, certain coordination tasks previously performed by people can be replaced by programs. Particular pieces of information trigger actions in the organization that are carried out even without the presence of the manager.

It is true that there are always attempts by members of the organization to subvert programs in order to expand their own scope for action. Overall, however, the organization is relieved of direct communication between managers and employees. The task of hierarchy is largely to ensure that the members of the organization are "willing to submit" to the rules (Luhmann 1964, p. 99).

In view of the possibility of using conditional and purpose-oriented programs to reduce the scope of decision-making and thus also leadership requirements, one can speak of leadership as an organization's gap filler (Luhmann 1971, p. 141). The activity required to carry out tasks is broken down into such small, standardized substeps and confined in such a tight technical and organizational corset that the need for leadership is greatly reduced. Leadership becomes a residual category for the formally nonprogrammable elements of the organization—any remaining ambiguities, monitoring compliance with rules, reacting to breakdowns, and dealing with deviations from the regulated process.

The Replacement of Management Requirements by Detailed Programming

The willingness of organizational practitioners to engage with Marxist theory is generally extremely low. In many cases, Karl Marx's own published works and those of his followers are not so simple that they can be understood without effort. There is often an assumption that critical analysis of the capitalist economy precludes the acquisition of practical knowledge about the functioning of organizations. This overlooks the fact that interesting insights into organizations can be gained from Marxist debates.

The Marxist debate on control through the design of work processes is instructive as regards the replacement of personal leadership by formal structures (for a detailed account of what follows, see Kühl 2019). The starting point for the labor process approach is the Marxian observation that capital employs two strategies to "get more out" of workers: the extension of working time without the capitalist having to pay more for it, and more effective use of purchased working time. These two strategies for increasing surplus value are interrelated. If the extension of working time is not possible due to legal rules for labor protection or collectively agreed working time regulations, "capital" will increase the intensity of work. The aim is to achieve optimum performance by improving technology and work organization. At the same time, too much intensity and too long working hours destroy the workforce. Therefore, an increase in the intensity of labor makes a reduction in working hours unavoidable (cf. Marx 1962, p. 440).

A prominent strand in Marxist analysis argues that increasingly prevalent rationalization strategies served to reshape the production process in such a way that experience, knowledge, and traditions of craftsmanship are no longer inextricably linked to the worker as a person. The knowledge that workers accumulated over decades and centuries was systematically shifted to management. This made the capitalist independent of the skills acquired by the worker and enabled the workforce to be completely subordinated to the goals, ideas, and plans of the management. Rationalization strategies allow the capitalist to kill two birds with one stone: firstly, they produce an efficient organizational structure thanks to which relative surplus value can be continuously increased; secondly, the deskilling of the workers and the drastic fragmentation of the work process enable better control of the workforce (cf. Braverman 1974, p. 124ff.).

This combination of rationalization and management control strategies is directly linked to a specific feature of the employment contract already outlined by Marx. Whereas a simple sales contract, for example, for the purchase of an electric scooter, a heat pump, or a jar of strawberry jam, specifies performance and consideration precisely, the employer only purchases labor in a very abstract form through an employment contract. By signing an employment contract, the employee issues a kind of "blank check" and agrees to use his labor, skills, and creativity in accordance with the task assigned to him. He refrains from specifying in detail what the work he performs is to consist of (cf. Commons 1924, p. 284).

This creates a control problem for the capitalist: while the employment contract specifies the employer's obligation precisely (namely the payment of wages), the employee's return obligation is not specified in detail. This means that the employee can try to evade the provision of services as much as possible. The purchase of labor power by the capitalist—the formal subsumption of the worker—is therefore not synonymous with the real use of labor power by capital—the real subsumption (cf. Marx 1962, p. 532f.). So, when the employer purchases labor power, he cannot be sure—unlike with any building, machine, or materials he purchases—that it can be smoothly integrated into the labor process (cf. Braverman 1974, p. 57; Friedman 1977, p. 78; Berger 1999, p. 155). Only through the systematic deskilling of workers and their subjugation to a Taylorist production regime can capitalists, according to the argument within the Marxist debate on labor processes, get this "transformation problem" of "abstract labor into real labor" under control to some extent (cf. Braverman 1974, p. 124ff.).

Marxist debates on labor processes argue against this position. Particularly in the face of rapidly changing markets and new technological developments, one strategy capital could adopt to solve the "transformation problem" would be to integrate workers into the production process by encouraging them to manage themselves. This strategy, which has been discussed in management literature under such terms as "the modular factory," "lean management," "business process reengineering," "the fractal factory," or "the agile organization," is captured in the Marxist debate on work processes by means of formulas such as "responsible autonomy," "flexible specialization," and "post-Fordist work organization."

This debate is interesting for a consideration of leadership requirements insofar as the concept of control is used to acknowledge that uncertainty of expectation in organizations can be reduced either through personal leadership or through formal structures. While "hierarchical control," according to the argument, relies heavily on direct personal leadership by superiors, "technical control"—and in a more subtle form, "bureaucratic control"—would work via work processes and targets that are specified in detail and thus reduce the need for personal leadership (for a distinction between the two, see Edwards 1979).

Replacing management tasks with programs can lead to an increase in efficiency in organizations. Organizations in which management relies exclusively on the control instrument of personal leadership as an element of coordination can only manage a low level of complexity, as leadership by people is based on communication via language. Although this is a central form of coordination and communication, it is also characterized by great complexity. If we had to clarify all transactions through linguistic communication only, we would still be talking about the question of our entry into nursery school as old men on our deathbeds

(Willke 1987, p. 139). Formalization and standardization through programs replace or reduce the need for personal guidance.

One of the benefits of conditional programs is that they relieve the hierarchy of the burden of making small-scale decisions, thus enabling it to preserve its capacity for planning and control. This is not done simply by issuing orders, but because authority is shifted to the information triggered by the conditional program. Authority is conferred on specific, selected information that moves the recipients to carry out a specified action. "Authority in this sense has shed all traditional conceptual qualities and consists merely in the communication of decision premises whose acceptance is motivated in a roundabout way, namely through system membership" (Luhmann 1964, p. 99). This makes every piece of information "authoritative" and every member of the organization, even an outsider, can become a "bearer" of this authority. "Routine and instruction are obviously two different, functionally equivalent forms of coordination, each of which has its particular advantages and disadvantages" (Luhmann 1971, p. 130). Conditional programs therefore protect the hierarchy. Conditional programming ensures that there are fewer situations in which uncertain expectations trigger the need for leadership.

One of the benefits of purpose-oriented programs is that they put "blinders" on the organization or parts of it (Luhmann 1973, p. 46). Goal setting leads to a considerable narrowing of an organization's horizons. It concentrates attention on a few aspects that appear important and ignores everything else. It is no longer necessary to fulfill every possible purpose, but only very specific ones. Each goal emphasizes certain aspects and neglects others. Purpose programs prevent organizations from being confused by a multitude of other possibilities. They can therefore reduce the number of uncertain situations and thus the need for leadership. A typical mechanism for this is strategy work. It creates a common goal orientation and thus, in principle, reduces basic negotiations about activities to be carried out.

In short: programs reduce managerial outlay because senior staff can withdraw from planning and control. Laterally, leadership is relieved because conditional programs enable impersonal action and authority is exercised not via the lateral leaders but via the programs themselves. Moreover, the need for supervision from below is also reduced because "the process" or "the strategy" prestructures the hierarchy's attention.

On the Replacement of Management by Programs: An Attempt at Target-Driven Control in a Media Company

In a large media company, different strategic orientations run counter to each other. In view of changing reading habits, there is a need for both high-quality journalism and new business models beyond daily and monthly newspapers. A strategic realignment was worked out in an elaborate strategizing process and rolled out across the various divisions. The increasingly digital business models and journalistic formats necessitated new forms of cooperation across editorial offices and divisions. In this respect, the aim was to switch to more agile management that would encourage cross-divisional collaboration.

With this aim in mind, objectives and key results were redefined throughout the organization. Specific targets—the objectives—were determined. These were often quantitative in nature—affecting such areas as sales development, product development cycles, and cost savings. Progress was recorded promptly on the basis of measurable outcomes—the key results. This method allowed for relatively small-scale management and process control as well as rapid adjustments, for example in the use of resources. The definition of objectives and key results was accompanied by a request typical of this method and intended to ensure the participation of those involved in the development: Tell us what you need to achieve the goal you've been set.

The set of objectives and key results introduced throughout the organization should in principle have contributed to a long-term overall strategy, but in fact led to a conspicuously short-cycle orientation. The organization quickly learned that anything that appeared on the list of objectives and key results would get management's attention and resources. As a result, more and more daily tasks ended up there. Alignment with a long-term overall strategy and orientation via the objectives and key results method came increasingly to diverge. Instead of the demands on management being reduced through a precise definition of objectives and key results, top management in particular had to constantly provide new leadership input in order to assert the overall strategy against the short-cycle orientation. It took a fundamental clarification by top management of how the overall strategy related to the objectives and key results to provide orientation and reduce the need for situational leadership.

However, like any form of organizing, relieving the burden of leadership through programs brings consequential problems Essentially, programs lack environmental sensitivity. Both purpose-oriented and conditional programs limit the organization's search area: a decision in favor of one purpose excludes the search for other purposes. Conditional programs obscure the view of other incoming information, leading, for example, to the organization becoming one-track-minded and less receptive to new stimuli from the environment. For example, the general social service work of youth welfare offices may become increasingly reliant on conditional programs for handling situations endangering the welfare of children. As a result, employees receive instructions on how to deal with difficult situations, and the organization is relieved of the burden of leadership. On the other hand, however, very different situations tend to get treated in the same way—and the experience possessed by long-standing employees may even be ignored. Conditional programs have the function of "safeguarding the precisest possible decision-making planning within the system against the vicissitudes of an uncontrollable environment that operates according to its own laws" (Luhmann 1971, p. 120). In this respect, the programs are the organization's answer to the contradiction between system autonomy and environmental dependency. The same applies to purpose-oriented programs, which make alternative needs in the environment difficult to observe due to their temporary nature.

Relieving the burden on the organization through programs therefore inevitably leads to a desensitization to problems. Both types of program anticipate the future to a certain extent and thus ensure the necessary reduction in complexity. After all, you can only program for both purpose and conditionality if you can anticipate what is coming towards you. For other futures that have not been programmed in advance, however, you have to fall back on leadership again.

3.2   Using Communication Channels to Relieve the Need for Leadership

Communication channels define legitimate points of contact and responsibilities. Initially, this massively restricts the possibilities for communication within the organization. It precludes a large number of possible contacts and the involvement of all potentially helpful and interested parties in decision making. Only a small number of legitimate contacts and authorized decision-makers are allowed, and members must respect these restrictions if they do not want to jeopardize their membership.

3.2.1   Different Forms of Communication Channels

There are different ways of regulating communication. The predominant way of defining communication channels is certainly through the hierarchy. Another important way is co-signing, which is also usually established via the hierarchy: Various ministers must agree before a regulation can come into force; department heads must countersign a work instruction before it can be officially promulgated in the organization. An increasingly important way of defining communication channels is by means of a project structure. Members from different departments are brought together to work on a temporary project—a special-purpose program. Hierarchies, co-signatory rights and project structures can be combined with one another, resulting in the development of very specific forms and networks of communication channels. Depending on which combination is chosen, the probability of cooperation, competition. or conflict in the organization changes.

On the Relationship Between Leadership and Hierarchy

A hierarchy is a set of fixed communication channels; leadership is a successful use of influence in a situation. To a certain extent, it could be described as a hierarchy within a situation. The exercise of hierarchy is clearly regulated, for example, by predefined processes, the authority to issue instructions, and the limits of what a manager is allowed to demand. What exactly leadership entails, on the other hand, cannot be determined in advance. It is not possible to predetermine who will come up with the cleverest idea in a meeting, who will convince everyone with their arguments, or whom the customer is going trust. Leadership, you might say, fills in the gaps in predictability.

Hierarchy is available at all times. Leadership only takes place at critical moments when organizational structures offer no direction and uncertainty arises. The exercise of hierarchy should be possible independently of people. Leadership, on the other hand, is attributed personally; it is an additional contribution to the system. Hierarchy uses formal powers to support the already established order. Leadership uses formal and informal means to enforce decisions. If you want to visualize the difference between hierarchy and leadership, hierarchy would be an established rail network, while leadership decides which path should be taken depending on the situation.

3.2.2 Communication Channels and Leadership

For the members of an organization, communication channels—like all other types of structure—have a relieving function. Those who are responsible for a particular decision can assume that it will be regarded as correct within the system and not be questioned. However, in the event of a problem, they will have to take responsibility and answer for any mistakes or negative consequences of their decision. This not only relieves the pressure on superiors, but also on subordinates, because they know whom they can and cannot talk to.

The idea behind channels of communication is, in particular, to reduce the number of possible contacts within an organization in order to reduce their complexity. Not everyone has to coordinate everything with everyone else. Organizations that rely on an extensive and well-developed hierarchy and a high degree of division of labor between the various levels in that hierarchy ensure clarity as to who has to report to whom and who has the say about what.

It is often mistakenly assumed that less hierarchy equals less leadership. However, the opposite is the case. The less an organization relies on hierarchy, the more leadership it needs, because when you remove the hierarchy, you remove a central point of orientation. The same applies if you do away with division of labor. If, in the interests of "cross-silo working" with the aid, for example, of initiatives involving more end-to-end responsibility, you strengthen cross-departmental cooperation, then the need for coordination and thus leadership increases.

The Replacement of Management by Communication Channels: A Case from an Engine Plant

An engine plant switched to self-organization. The workers on each shop floor were divided into so-called cluster groups, each of which organized itself without a foreman. The groups decided on the work processes, the skills required, allocation to different tasks within the shift—as well as on rostering for shifts and the distribution of vacation time. Problems in the work process, with other clusters or with the control of production were clarified by a spokesperson for the cluster with those affected. The spokespersons had no hierarchical authority.

After some time, the dysfunctional consequences of the reduction in hierarchy became apparent. In some clusters, there was an increase in the number of conflict situations because the members were unable to resolve disputes regarding shift scheduling or taking leave. In other clusters, the cluster spokespersons also took over shift rostering and vacation planning in addition to their role as the cluster's "exterior minister." With varying degrees of success in each case. Internal planning took up a lot of time. The lack of hierarchical decision-making authority had to be compensated for by leadership. How well this worked in each case depended heavily on the people involved.

After a few months, the plant management also recognized the structural problems and subsequently gave the spokespeople hierarchical authority. Self-organization was eliminated at least to the extent that less time-consuming management work was required within the teams.

Communication channels can reduce the need for leadership, but they also determine where disputes are likely to occur. In a functional organization, in which each function (e.g. marketing, production, or sales) is a separate department, the communication channels create a silo-like work situation so that for overarching projects, such as the introduction of a joint computer program, coordination problems are almost inevitable. Under these conditions, the structures provide little certainty of expectation, so leadership is necessary. In a matrix organization, on the other hand, which has grown out of the idea of preventing the formation of silos, doubt about responsibilities quickly arises at the "nodes" of the matrix. Here leadership may be necessary in order to make situational decisions about the "dual orientation" created by the matrix arrangement.

Communication channels not only substitute for leadership efforts, they also create follow-up problems in the shape of a constant need for further leadership. From an organizational design perspective, it is therefore important to ask whether the leadership requirements that communication channels create lead to constructive tensions, for example, because conflicts over resources do not get decided once and for all, and whether the requirements arrive at the right place, and appropriate means of exerting an influence are available there.

3.3   Reducing the Need for Leadership Through Decisions Regarding Personnel

On the basis of the concept of organizational structures explained above, it is easy to demonstrate the structural character of decisions about personnel. Any observer can see that, in organizations, not only are decisions made about personnel, but that personnel decisions are important premises for further decisions made within the organization. It makes a difference to future decisions who occupies the position responsible for making the decision. Put in the same position, lawyers will often make different decisions from business economists, who in turn will make different decisions from sociologists.

3.3.1 Various Ways of Influencing Staff

Organizations have various options for adjusting "personnel" parameters. Hiring determines the type of people who will make decisions in the organization in the future. Even when formulating job advertisements, candidate profiles, and any supporting documents, there is a fierce battle to determine which characteristics—and thus ultimately which decision-making styles relevant to the organization—an applicant should bring to the table. Dismissing staff can signal the kind of decisions you no longer want to have in the organization in the future. Internal transfers can go upwards, downwards, or even sideways. Staff development, on the other hand, is often simply aimed at changing people's behavior so that they make different decisions in the same position in the future.

3.3.2 Personnel and Leadership

The decision as to who will make which decisions from now on, i.e., how a position is to be actually filled, has a major impact on the leadership requirements in organizations. If the expectations the organization has of people are highly standardized, it is possible to predict with reasonable accuracy how the staff member in question will probably decide. Situations where expectations are uncertain will be reduced as a result, and so will the need for leadership.

This reduction in the need for leadership can be observed in organizations that systematically recruit the same type of people and take a lot of trouble to socialize the new members in the organization. If a development bank systematically recruits only economists with good language skills who have done internships abroad, trains them from day one of their employment to write perfect program proposals for development aid projects, and binds them to the organization for the long term, it can assume that its members will think and act similarly. This reduces the need for leadership.

This reduction in the need for leadership can also be observed in organizations that largely fill their top management positions with long-serving members. Their top people will be comparatively predictable because everyone knows what makes them tick. There is a high degree of certainty of expectation in the organization. If, however, the top personnel are recruited from outside in order to bring a breath of fresh air into the organization, the degree of leadership required increases, especially so far as their immediate colleagues are concerned. The new managers will need to be steered from below by a variety of leadership maneuvers so that they do not upset the organizational setup too much. But since they are often likely to object to this kind of leading—after all, they were brought in to do things differently—there is often quite a lot of tugging to and from within the organization as a result.

Challenges to Leadership Where One Has a Limited Hold Over Personnel: An Example from Academia

The central lever for influencing the way decisions are made in academic organizations is the appointment of professors. The reason for this is that there are limited opportunities for influencing professors once they have been appointed. This becomes clear when you look at how little effect can be had on them via communication channels and programs.

Although academic organizations have hierarchical communication channels, their access to individual professors is very limited. While professors have very far-reaching influence over their employees, because they not only decide on the renewal of their contracts, but also review the work they do to qualify for their positions, university presidents and rectors have only very limited influence on them. Professors are protected by lifelong contracts and by the constitution with regard to guaranteed freedom of research. Some professors are even surprised to be told that they have official superiors.

Professors can also only be controlled to a very limited extent via programs. Conditional programs may be suitable for controlling such things as travel expense accounting, personnel recruitment processes, and curricula, but cannot be used to set content-related guidelines. Control via special-purpose programs can be attempted by offering professors the prospect of bonuses if they participate in the department's research projects, but they cannot be directly ordered to do so.

This is particularly evident in academic institutions that appoint researchers who are considered to be excellent to head up departments and then allow them to work largely at will. The pressure of expectations is often so great that the head of department passes it on to the employees. In order to make good the expectations of the institution's top management, means are often used that are regarded by employees as bullying, but against which they can only defend themselves with difficulty due to their limited contracts. If the problems become public under the label of an abuse of power, there are only very limited possibilities for the supervisory authorities to intervene because the opportunities for direct instruction and monitoring are limited.

The idea of using personnel as a decision-making premise becomes plausible if you consider how much is "organized around" certain people in organizations. You anticipate how a particular person is likely to react and act accordingly, for example by not putting forward certain ideas in the first place or even by aligning your position with theirs. While it is easy to alter decisions regarding what is to be expected of formal roles, expectations placed on individuals are generally very difficult to change. Even if the person concerned asserts that he or she will no longer make the same demands as before, expectations often remain stable for a long time. In contrast to substitution by communication channels and programs, using personnel to replace leadership leads to the organization's becoming dependent on individuals. A change in the people who are central to the organization may, for example, create discontinuities that are not so easy to compensate for with new staff.

3.4   Influencing the Need for Leadership by Working on the Structures of the Organization

To visualize the ways in which organizations influence leadership, imagine the three structural elements—programs, communication channels, and personnel—as being like controls on a mixing console. On the left-hand side of the mixer is a switch that is used to set whether the focus is on the show, the formal, or the informal side. Because the formal structure is usually the starting point for changes in the organization, the lever is set "by default" to the formal side. On the right-hand side, there are controls that can be used

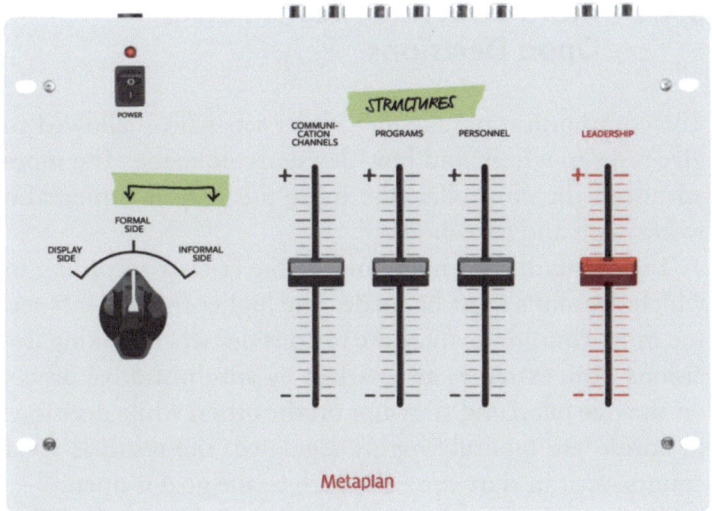

Fig. 3.1 The management console

to adjust the extent to which formal expectations are influenced by communication channels, programs, and personnel. If the slider is high, this type of structure plays a major role in the formulating formal expectations; if it is low, it plays a minor one (Fig. 3.1).

Extending the management mixer to take leadership requirements into account is done by adding a slider that displays the level of leadership an organization needs. If the formal expectations connected with communication channels, programs, and personnel are specified very precisely, leadership requirements will be low and the slider will drop into the minus range. If the formal expectations are less precisely specified, the expectations of leadership requirements will be significantly higher and the slider will move upwards.

3.4.1 More Structure Means Fewer Open Decisions

The communication channels slider sets who is allowed to give tasks to whom and how decisions are made. The more advanced the controller, the more precisely it limits who works with and for whom.

The program controller bundles the criteria according to which decisions must be made. The higher this slider is set, the more conditions there are to consider when making decisions. The extremes are marked by administrative offices on the one hand and start-ups on the other: while decisions in admin are typically highly regulated, the result is what counts most in start-ups. The path to the goal is open.

The personnel regulator determines the degree of differentiation as to which staff members in the organization can fill which positions. This regulator is pushed to the maximum in some family businesses, for example. You will have the best chance of making a career there if you happen to be the child of the current boss. Qualifications, time with the company, or experience in the relevant area only count to a certain degree.

The primary focus with respect to recruitment is the formal structure of the organization. However, informal expectations can also generate certainty of expectation. They usually creep in when someone takes the lead and establishes a deviation from an existing procedure.

3.4.2 What Happens When You Move the Controls?

If you want to use the mixing console effectively, asking a few questions will help. The first step is to check: How are the controls set in my organization? Is it clear who works with whom or does this vary a lot? Is the way you fulfill an assignment either right or wrong or is there something else that we use as a guide?

After taking stock, the central questions as regards change projects are: Which controls can be moved at all—and by whom? For example, is it possible to relax the conditions under which the programs operate and allow new ways of solving tasks? Has a new strategy just been rolled out that stands in the way of further change?

Another key question is: What happens when you move the controls? In other words: How will the organization react? Who will welcome and support this? What resistance should we expect and how can we counter it? If you consider this in advance, you have a much better chance of reacting quickly and effectively later on!

3.4.3 Leadership: The Final Amplifier of the Organizational Signal

In addition to the structural controls, organizations have another special control on the mixer: the intensity of organizational leadership. We do not understand leadership as a synonym for hierarchy, but rather as the assertion of open decision-making, the resolution of contradictions, and the maintenance of certainty of expectation. This means that everyone, not just superiors, can take the lead—as long as their actions carry conviction and generate followers.

You can think of leadership as a power amplifier that brings all the signals coming out of the mixing console to the same level. How much leadership is required depends on the position of the structural controls. If they are set higher, leadership is less necessary and less effective. Conversely, if the structural level is low, more decisions need to be made on the basis of leadership in individual cases.

3.4.4 Why the Management Console?

The management console takes a vast amount of complexity out of organizations. Communication channels, programs, and personnel are not influenced by a single controller, but by a multitude of controllers. You only have to look at how the basic hierarchical structure of communication channels is attenuated by various co-signing rights, project structures, and voting committees. The representation of controls as plus and minus scales is a gross oversimplification, because the concept of formal expectation formation can only be illustrated on the basis of more or less of different elements by leaving so many things out. It needs an explanation at the very least, which is why, for example, a detailed definition of professional standards for doctors and lawyers requires a precise definition of formal principles. Even so, despite all its drawbacks owing to the considerable simplification of organizational reality involved, the management console does make it possible to get a clear picture of the connection between formal structure and management requirements on the basis of concrete problems.

Dealing with Frustration Caused by Limited Influence as a Manager in a Retail Company

Large retail companies with salaried store managers are characterized by the fact that work in their branches is very strictly regulated by programs. They specify down to the smallest detail which goods are to be kept in stock, how the shelves are to be positioned, and what prices are to be charged. Even if it might make sense for a store manager to position surplus pallets of strawberries directly beside the checkouts for impulse buying in summer, this is strictly forbidden by the program, which stipulates that strawberries must always be positioned in the fruit and vegetable section (for a precise insider report, see Straub 2012).

Compliance with this program is ensured by a strict hierarchical structure consisting of sales management, area management, and branch management. Area management, which is responsible for a dozen branches or so, monitors whether the branch managers strictly adhere to the programs. If it regularly identifies deviations, it is required to first warn the branch manager and then dismiss him or her. The ability to enforce precise adherence to the program by dismissing store managers is seen as a key qualification for managers at area level.

When recruiting branch and area managers, care is taken to ensure that the management personnel are able to deal with this strict programming and sophisticated hierarchical communication channels. Managers who have previously been in the army are particularly popular recruits because, on the one hand, they are used to strictly programmed organizations and, on the other, are trained to have instructions that are passed down the hierarchy carried out by their own subordinates. This results in a high degree of homogeneity in terms of a company's management personnel. While branch employees receive rather low salaries, care is taken to ensure that people at management level are well paid in order to attract and retain quality staff through financial motivation.

Branch managers' authority is limited to enforcing detailed programs for product placement, price labeling, and checkout procedures while keeping the costs for the deployment of personnel as low as possible. In addition to precise conditional programs, their behavior is thus shaped by a purpose program that gives them freedom in the matter of personnel deployment. Because personnel costs are the only lever that can be used to influence the profit made by a branch, managers have a strong incentive to calculate outlay on staff as tightly as possible and to get as much as possible out of the available workforce.

Using the management console model, it is possible to make it clear to area and branch managers in retail groups how limited their expectations and options as regards leadership actually are. Retail group executives who work with the management console set the controls for communication channels, programs, and personnel very high in workshops. Because the leadership control mechanism correlates with those for communication channels, programs, and personnel, it is soon obvious how few leadership opportunities exist. Leadership requirements largely consist of enforcing detailed programs on potentially erratic or resistant employees.

When working with top management, the management mixer can be used to illustrate that management requirements change as soon as managers move out of the core operational area of sales. Senior managers in administration, purchasing, store development, and logistics, in particular, do not have the same formal security of expectations as managers in sales. This can be seen by the fact that they set the controls for communication channels, programs, and personnel far lower down the scale in workshops than their colleagues in sales. By visualizing the discrepancy, it is possible to discuss what other requirements are necessary for leadership in these areas.

The management mixer can be applied to specific problems in organizations through a series of guiding questions. The question of where the sliders currently stand on the communication channels, programs, and personnel scales might prompt a discussion about the degree of formal expectations in the organization. The question of which sliders could be shifted could draw attention to where the starting points for changes to the formal structure might lie. The question of what happens when a regulator is changed can make it clear how changes in, for example, the qualifications needed by staff, would affect requirements for programs and communication channels to be formally fixed. The question of what else might be needed because the formal structures alone do not provide sufficient guidance might turn the focus onto the connection between organizational structures and leadership requirements.

Good organizing means asking yourself and others: In which areas of the organization do we need openness for decisions to be made by management on a case-by-case basis? Which areas, on the other hand, need a fixed structure in order to reduce the time and effort spent on leadership? What problems does this entail? The mixing desk invites reflection on what the organization needs and what role leadership plays, or should play, in it. It also makes it possible to explain the recurring need for leadership on certain issues and—if it is not possible to build structures—to prepare more specifically for these recurring, critical moments.

It makes sense to question the desire for more leadership more often, not only to reduce some of the demands placed on managers, but, above all, to actually respond to uncertain situations with more certainty. With the help of three questions, organizations can test their problems and any undecided issues to see whether leadership—and not structure—could really be the solution for them: Were there previously solutions based on rules or routines? How did these get lost? Is there a repeating pattern in the ways such situations are resolved and could this pattern become a fixed process? Or: do you want this problem to be brought back to the table again and again because you need the flexibility given by leadership that is lacking in structures? And who should be given leadership in such situations? Do these people have the necessary means of influence?

4

Organizing Leadership: A Plea

Because it is impossible to create certainty of expectations for every situation, a need for leadership will inevitably arise. The good news, however, is that leadership needs can be anticipated and managed within certain limits. So, organizations will always remain dependent on leadership—but can use structure to significantly influence how leadership needs and opportunities are distributed. In principle, any member of the organization can take the lead—from the top down, from the bottom up, or from the side.

In discussions on leadership, however, the spotlight has so far not been on organizations, but on people, who appear in the shape of efficient managers, as leaders who take you off to one side or clever 'underseers' of their superiors, like stopgaps for problems left behind by the formal structure. Difficulties in the organization are quickly assigned to the category of problems caused by a lack of leadership on the part of those in charge. On the basis of this logic, staff are taken in hand through assessment centers and personnel development measures, placed under a moral obligation

© The Author(s), under exclusive license to Springer Nature Switzerland AG 2025
S. Kühl, J. Muster, *Managing Leadership*,
https://doi.org/10.1007/978-3-032-09268-7_4

through concepts such as transformational leadership, or replaced on account of obvious leadership deficits.

In many organizations, there is a tendency to attribute unresolved problems to the staff. The individual appears as a "catch-all" for "organizationally unsolved—perhaps unsolvable—problems" (Luhmann 2018, p. 236). This is why there is a massive need for something to lean on in person-oriented methods. The function of a large part of leadership training and leadership literature is to satisfy this "need to find something to lean on." Resilience training, coaching in conflict management, or a book on intercultural leadership can be brought in quickly and easily and leads to reassurance in the organization because something is being done.

However, this focus on person-centered solutions is always a risk in organizations. The hope of being able to solve their structural problems by means of personnel selection and development procedures is usually overoptimistic and therefore often leads to frustration. Especially in middle management positions, staff are frequently prone to burn out because the organization is reluctant to address its structural problems. This often leads to increased staff turnover, which in turn makes it increasingly difficult for the organization to build up the knowledge it needs to tackle those problems.

Contrary to these trends, a systems theory perspective attempts to open our eyes to the idea that, with respect to the demands for leadership made on them, people can, within certain limits, be "relieved by better organization" (Luhmann 2018, p. 236). Anyone who wants to talk about leadership ought not, therefore, to pass over organization in silence.

References

Alvesson, Mats. 2013. The Triumph of Emptiness: Consumption, Higher Education, and Work Organization. Oxford, New York: Oxford University Press.

Alvesson, Mats, and André Spicer. 2014. "Critical Perspectives on Leadership." In the Oxford Handbook of Leadership and Organizations, edited by David V. Day, 40–56. Oxford: Oxford University Press.

Bass, Bernard M. 1985. Leadership and Performance Beyond Expectations. New York: Free Press.

Bavelas, Alex. 1960. "Leadership: Man and Function." Administrative Science Quarterly 4: 491–98.

Berger, Johannes. 1999. "Der Konsensbedarf der Wirtschaft." In Die Wirtschaft der modernen Gesellschaft, edited by Johannes Berger, 155–94. Frankfurt a.M., New York: Campus.

Bing, Stanley. 2004. What Would Machiavelli Do? The Ends Justify the Meanness. New York: HarperCollins.

Braverman, Harry. 1974. Labor and Monopoly Capital: The Degradation of Work in the Twentieth Century. New York, London: Monthly Review Press.

© The Author(s), under exclusive license to Springer Nature Switzerland AG 2025
S. Kühl, J. Muster, *Managing Leadership*,
https://doi.org/10.1007/978-3-032-09268-7

References

Burns, Tom, and George M. Stalker. 1961. The Management of Innovation. London: Tavistock.

Ciborra, Claudio. 1996. "The Platform Organization: Recombining Strategies, Structures, and Surprises." Organization Science 7: 103–18.

Commons, John R. 1924. Legal Foundation of Capitalism. New York: Macmillan.

Crozier, Michel, and Erhard Friedberg. 1977. L'acteur et le système. Paris: Seuil.

Drucker, Peter F. 1982. The Changing World of the Executive. New York: Truman Talley Books.

Edwards, Richard C. 1979. Contested Terrain. New York: Basic Books.

Friedman, Andrew. 1977. Industry and Labour. London: Macmillan.

Gemmill, Gary, and Judith Oakley. 1992. "Leadership: An Alienating Social Myth?" Human Relations 45: 113–29.

Goleman, Daniel, Richard E. Boyatzis, and Annie McKee. 2013. Primal Leadership: Unleashing the Power of Emotional Intelligence. Boston: Harvard Business School Press.

Jachtchenko, Wladislaw. 2021. The 5 Roles of Leadership: Tools & Best Practices for Personable and Effective Leaders. Oakland Park: Remote Verlag.

Jay, Anthony. 1968. Management and Machiavelli. New York: Hodder and Stoughton.

Kerr, Steven. 1977. "Substitutes for Leadership: Some Implications for Organizational Design." Organization and Administrative Sciences 8: 135–46.

Kerr, Steven, and J.M Jermier. 1978. "Substitutes for Leadership: Their Meaning and Measurement." Organizational Behavior and Human Performance 22: 375–403.

Kotter, John P. 1990. "What Leaders Really Do." Harvard Business Review (3): 103–11.

Kouzes, James M., and Barry Z. Posner. 2017. The Leadership Challenge: How to Make Extraordinary Dhings Happen in Organizations. 6th ed. Hoboken: Wiley.

Kühl, Stefan. 2017. Lateral Leading: A Very Brief Introduction to Power, Understanding and Trust. Princeton, Hamburg, Shanghai, Singapore, Versailles, Zurich: Organizational Dialogue Press.

Kühl, Stefan. 2019. Work: Marxist and Systems-Theoretical Approaches. London, New York: Routledge.

Kühl, Stefan. 2021. Organizations: A Short Introduction. Princeton, Hamburg, Shanghai, Singapore, Versailles, Zurich: Organizational Dialogue Press.

Kühl, Stefan. 2023. Shadow Organizations: Agile Management and Unwanted Bureaucratization. Princeton, Hamburg, Shanghai, Singapore, Versailles, Zurich: Organizational Dialogue Press.

Lakomski, Gabriele. 2005. Managing Without Leadership: Towards a Theory of Organizational Functioning. Amsterdam, Boston, Paris: Emerald Group.

Lalich, Janja. 2004. Bounded Choice: True Believers and Charismatic Cults. Berkeley: University of California Press.

Laloux, Frederic. 2014. Reinventing Organizations: A Guide to Creating Organizations Inspired by the Next Stage of Human Consciousness. Brussels: Nelson Parker.

Lawrence, Paul R., and Jay W. Lorsch. 1967. Organization and Environment: Managing Differentiation and Integration. Homewood: Irwin.

Locke, Edwin A. 2003. "Foundation of a Theory of Leadership." In the Future of Leadership, edited by Susan E. Murphy and Ronald E. Riggio, 29–46. Mahwah: Erlbaum.

Luhmann, Niklas. 1964. Funktionen und Folgen formaler Organisation. Berlin: Duncker & Humblot.

Luhmann, Niklas. 1971. "Lob der Routine." In Politische Planung, edited by Niklas Luhmann, 113–43. Opladen: WDV.

Luhmann, Niklas. 1973. Zweckbegriff und Systemrationalität. Frankfurt a.M. Suhrkamp.

Luhmann, Niklas. 2000. Organisation und Entscheidung. Opladen: WDV.

References

Luhmann, Niklas. 2016. "Unterwachung oder die Kunst, Vorgesetzte zu lenken." In Der Neue Chef, edited by Jürgen Kaube, 90–106. Berlin: Suhrkamp.

Luhmann, Niklas. 2018. "Die Bedeutung der Organisationssoziologie für Betrieb und Unternehmung." In Schriften zur Organisation 1: Die Wirklichkeit der Organisation, edited by Niklas Luhmann, 231–54. Wiesbaden: Springer VS.

Machiavelli, Niccolò. 1955. Der Fürst. Stuttgart: Kröner.

March, James G., and Herbert A. Simon. 1958. Organizations. New York: John Wiley & Sons.

Marx, Karl. 1962. "Das Kapital: Erstes Buch." In Marx-Engels-Werke: Band 23, edited by Karl Marx, 11–955. Berlin: Dietz.

McAlpine, Alistair. 2000. The New Machiavelli: The Art of Politics in Business. New York, Chichester: Wiley.

McCann, Leo. 2015. "From Management to Leadership." In the SAGE Handbook of the Sociology of Work and Employment, edited by Stephen Edgell, Heidi Gottfried, and Edward Granter, 167–84. London: Sage.

Micklethwait, John, and Adrian Wooldridge. 1996. The Witch Doctors: Making Sense of the Management Gurus. London: William Heinemann.

Miner, John B. 1975. "The Uncertain Future of the Leadership Concept: An Overview." In Leadership Frontiers, edited by James G. Hunt and Lars L. Larson, 197–208. Kent: Kent State University Press.

Mintzberg, Henry, and Alexandra McHugh. 1985. "Strategy Formation in an Adhocracy." Administrative Science Quarterly 30: 180–97.

Morgan, Gareth. 1986. Images of Organization. Beverly Hills: Sage.

Neuberger, Oswald. 2002. Führen und führen lassen: Ansätze, Ergebnisse und Kritik der Führungsforschung. 6th ed. Stuttgart: Lucius & Lucius.

Nutzinger, Hans G. 1979. "Uncertainty, Hierarchy and Vertical Integration." Economic Analysis and Workers' Management 13: 301–25.

Peters, Thomas J. 1993. Jenseits der Hierarchien: Liberation Management. Düsseldorf: Econ.

Pfeffer, Jeffrey. 1977. "The Ambiguity of Leadership." The Academy of Management Review 2: 104–12.

Simon, Herbert A. 1957. Administrative Behavior. 2nd ed. New York: The Free Press.

Staehle, Wolfgang H. 1985. Management: Eine verhaltenswissenschaftliche Einführung. 2nd ed. München: Vahlen.

Stogdill, Ralph M. 1974. Handbook of Leadership: A Survey of Theory and Research. New York: Free Press.

Straub, Andreas. 2012. Aldi - einfach billig: Ein ehemaliger Manager packt aus. Reinbek bei Hamburg: Rowohlt.

Toffler, Alvin. 1971. Future Shock. New York: Bantam Book.

Türk, Klaus. 1981. Personalführung und soziale Kontrolle. Stuttgart: Enke.

Türk, Klaus. 1987. "Entpersonalisierte Führung." In Handwörterbuch der Führung, edited by Alfred Kieser, Gerhard Reber, and Rolf Wunderer, 231–41. Stuttgart: Schäffer-Poeschel.

Weber, Max. 1976. Wirtschaft und Gesellschaft. Tübingen: J.C.B. Mohr.

Willke, Helmut. 1987. Systemtheorie: Eine Einführung in die Grundprobleme. Stuttgart, New York: Fischer UTB.

Witzel, Morgen. 2012. A History of Management Thought. London: Routledge.

Yukl, Gary. 1999. "An Evaluative Essay on Current Conceptions of Effective Leadership." European Journal of Work and Organizational Psychology 8: 33–48.

Zaleznik, Abraham. 1977. "Managers and Leaders: Are They Different?" Harvard Business Review 5: 67–80.

Zaleznik, Abraham. 1989. The Managerial Mystique: Restoring Leadership in Business. New York: Harper & Row.